THE SECRET LIFE OF VIRUSES

INCREDIBLE SCIENCE FACTS ABOUT GERMS, VACCINES, AND WHAT YOU CAN DO TO STAY HEALTHY

MARIONA TOLOSA SISTERÉ
THE ELLAS EDUCAN COLLECTIVE

We know that viruses exist, but they are so tiny that they can't be seen with the naked eye.

Viruses have a very bad reputation, but only a few of them actually cause disease in humans.

Viruses are capable of doing extraordinary things such as helping to keep our planet's ecology balanced and getting rid of dangerous organisms.

ENEMY CELL

BACTERIUM

VIRUSES ARE MADE UP OF:

1 DNA OR RNA

This is the genetic material that contains all the information viruses need in order to reproduce.

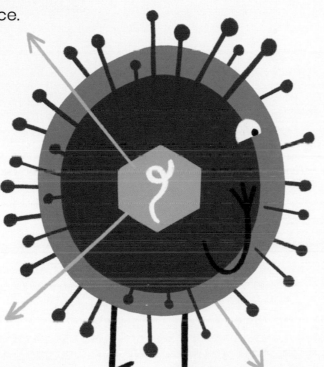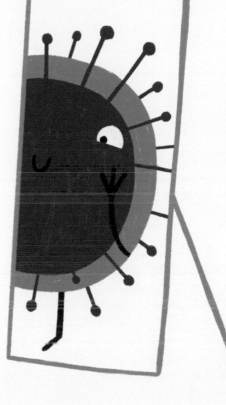

2 CAPSID

This is a shell made of proteins that protects the DNA or RNA.

3 ENVELOPE

This is a layer of fat (also called lipids) with protein accessories that covers them like a suit. Viruses' envelopes can take thousands of different shapes and forms, and some viruses don't have envelopes.

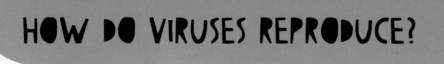

HOW DO VIRUSES REPRODUCE?

Viruses are unusual because they can only reproduce inside cells by infecting them. Cells are the basic units of all living organisms such as bacteria, plants, animals, and humans like you.

What's up? I think we've met before. I'm the virus that causes the common cold. Watch what happens when I infect you!

RHINOVIRUS

BIRD FLU

BACTERIOPHAGE

1 First I enter your body through your nose or mouth. Here I go!

A **BACTERIUM** is a living organism made up of a single cell. Not to be mistaken for a virus!

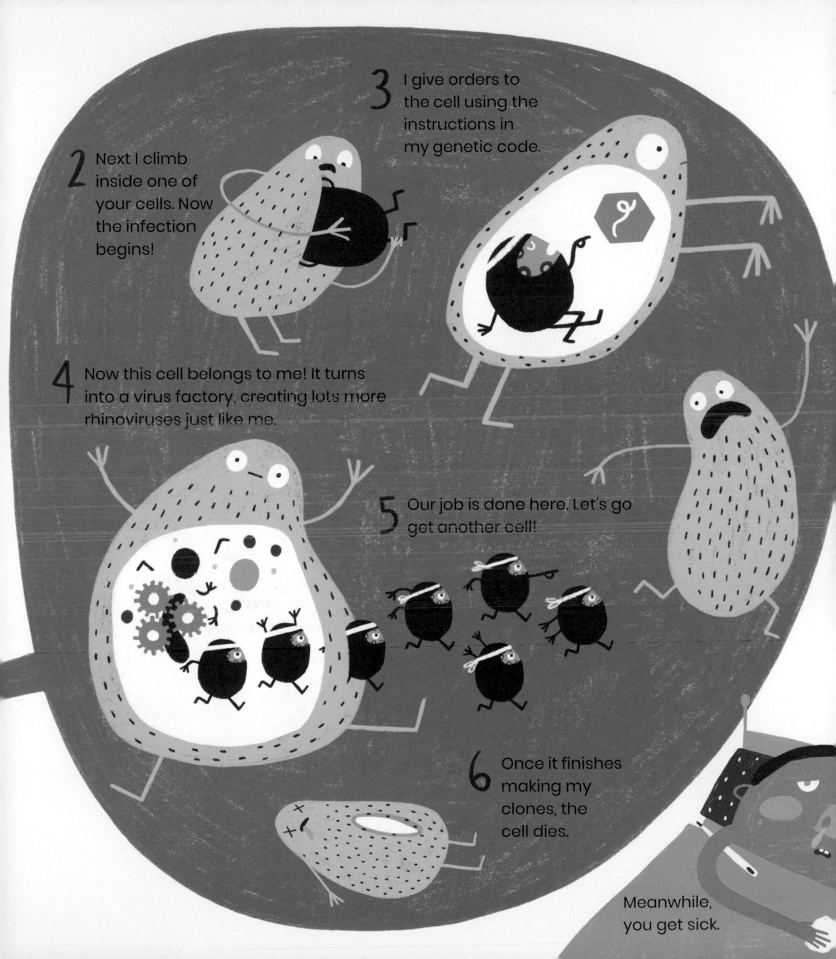

CATALOG OF VIRUSES

*An asterisk denotes there is a vaccine to defeat that virus.

BACTERIOPHAGE

Our body is full of viruses, and most of them coexist peacefully with the good bacteria in our body.

WHAT'S UP?

RABIES*

I am very bad and spread through bites from wild animals.

HERPES SIMPLEX VIRUS (HSV)

I cause cold sores. I'm pretty harmless but very common—I've infected more than half of all humans around the world!

SARS-COV-2 (NOVEL CORONAVIRUS)*

Like it or not, you know who I am.

RHINOVIRUS

Hello again! So many boogers! Achoo!

VARICELLA ZOSTER*

I give kids chicken pox, which can make you very itchy! But there's a vaccine that can keep me from infecting you.

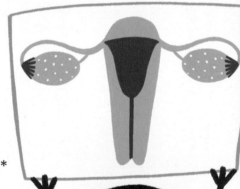

VARIOLA*

I cause smallpox. I used to be very dangerous, but humans managed to get rid of me with vaccines.

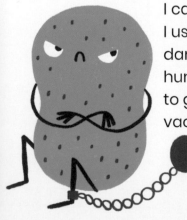

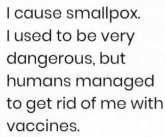

HUMAN PAPILLOMA VIRUS (HPV)*

I can be dangerous to women, but I grow very slowly which means doctors can detect me before I can make someone sick!

DENGUE

Are you in the tropics? Be careful around mosquitoes. They carry me from one person to another.

HUMAN IMMUNODEFICIENCY VIRUS (HIV)

I attack and weaken your body's defense system, which can make you very sick over time.

EBOLA*

I am a really bad virus. I infect humans and other primates, such as monkeys, gorillas, and chimpanzees and make them very, very sick.

INFLUENZA*

I'm always reinventing myself. Every year a new "me" appears.

ONCOLYTIC VIRUS

I can be helpful. I try to catch and kill cancer cells.

SUPERBACTERIOPHAGE

Some bad bacteria might survive antibiotics, but they're no match for me!

ROTAVIRUS*

Diarrhea? Nausea? Stomachache? That's me!

ANTIBIOTIC RESISTANT BACTERIA

UH-OH, A VIRUS GOT IN!

A rotavirus has managed to reach your intestines! Your immune system, led by white blood cells, is responsible for fighting viruses like these.

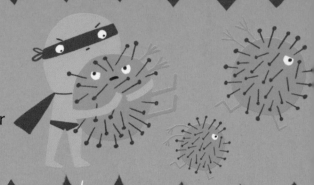

INTESTINAL MUCUS

2 ADAPTIVE RESPONSE

More and more white blood cells join the fight.

ANTIBODIES

3 VICTORY!

Your immune system has won the battle.

B LYMPHOCYTES

They help produce proteins called antibodies that specialize in identifying and eliminating viruses.

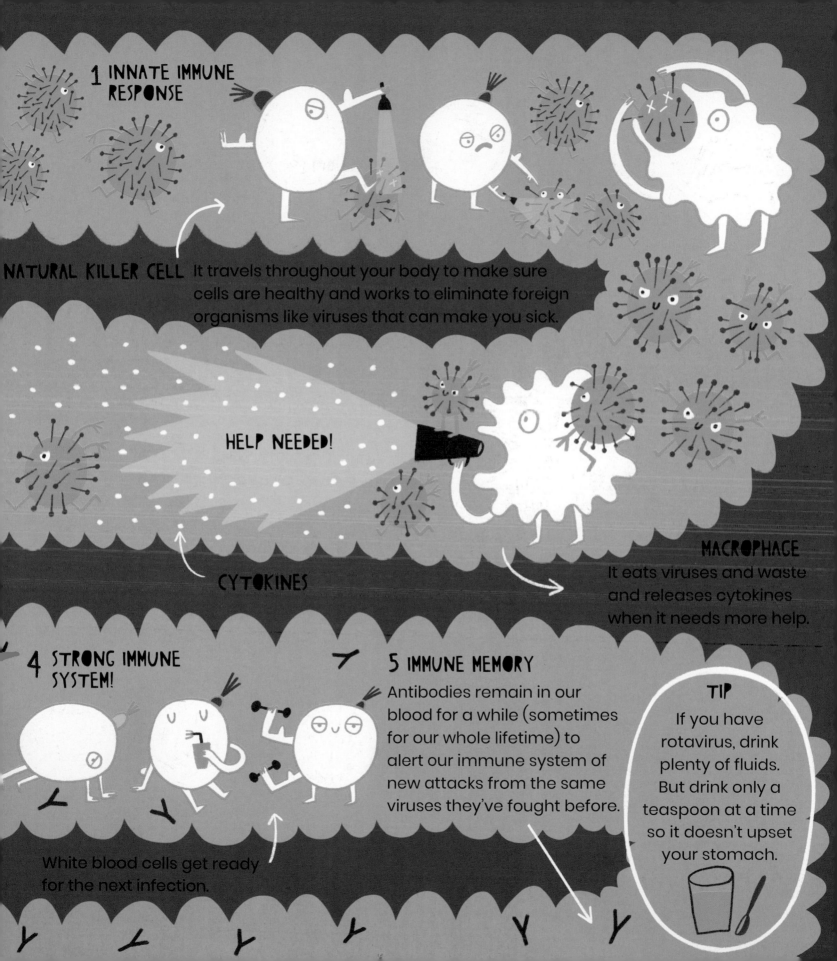

HOW DO VIRUSES SPREAD?

Viruses spread in lots of different ways. Fortunately, medications and vaccines help us fight infection.

The **FLU** virus stays on some surfaces for hours. Make sure to wash your hands often!

Sneezing can spread the **RHINOVIRUS**.

Don't rub your eyes with dirty hands. You might contract **ADENOVIRUS** and then get pink eye!

Female mosquitoes can transmit the **DENGUE** virus.

Ticks can transmit **POWASSAN** virus which can make you very sick. Keep an eye out!

ROTAVIRUS spreads through contaminated poop. Make sure to wash your hands after you use the bathroom to avoid getting gastroenteritis (stomach flu).

When you get the **VARICELA-ZOSTER** virus, you get a rash all over that itches a lot!

Vaccines help us create the antibodies necessary to kill viruses. They often contain weakened viruses that teach our bodies how to fight that virus!

WHAT IS A PANDEMIC?

Hey! How's it going? My name is SARS-COV-2 and I am the coronavirus responsible for COVID-19. I spread super fast and in just a few months I managed to infect humans all over the world—I caused a pandemic!

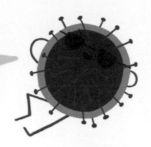

While scientists worked hard to develop a vaccine to defeat me, lots of people stayed at home to avoid me and keep me from spreading to more people.

EXPONENTIAL GROWTH

If each infected person infects more than one person, the number of transmissions grows faster and faster.

EXHAUSTED MEDICAL STAFF

CROWDED HOSPITALS

CLOSED SCHOOLS

STAYING HEALTHY

What can you do to stay safe from viruses?

1 Eat healthy foods, like fruits and vegetables.

2 Try not to touch your face (especially your eyes, nose, and mouth) with your hands.

3 If you sneeze or cough and you don't have a tissue, sneeze into your elbow.

4 Wash your hands with soap and warm water often and make sure to scrub for at least 20 seconds.

5 Wear a mask when you leave the house. When you protect yourself, you are also protecting those around you!

6 Maintain a proper social distance from others.

6 FEET

7 Keep your immune system strong by exercising regularly.

VIRUSES AND OUR PLANET

Most viruses on Earth reproduce in bacteria cells. Bacteria are crucial to the cycle of life on Earth and can even influence the climate. By infecting bacteria, viruses also play a very important role in the ecosystems of our planet.

In a drop of water on the surface of the ocean, you can find up to 10 million viruses!

Some viruses control the growth of algae made up of a kind of bacteria called cyanobacteria.

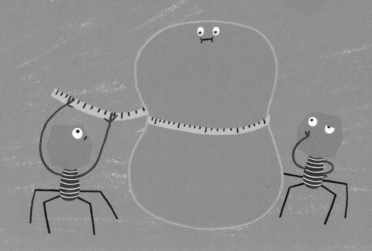

Viruses also reproduce in fungi, plants, and animals.

The **CURVULARIA THERMAL TOLERANCE VIRUS** infects fungi in plants and makes them resistant to high temperatures.

TOMATO SPOTTED WILT VIRUS

TULIP BREAKING VIRUS

PAPAYA RINGSPOT VIRUS

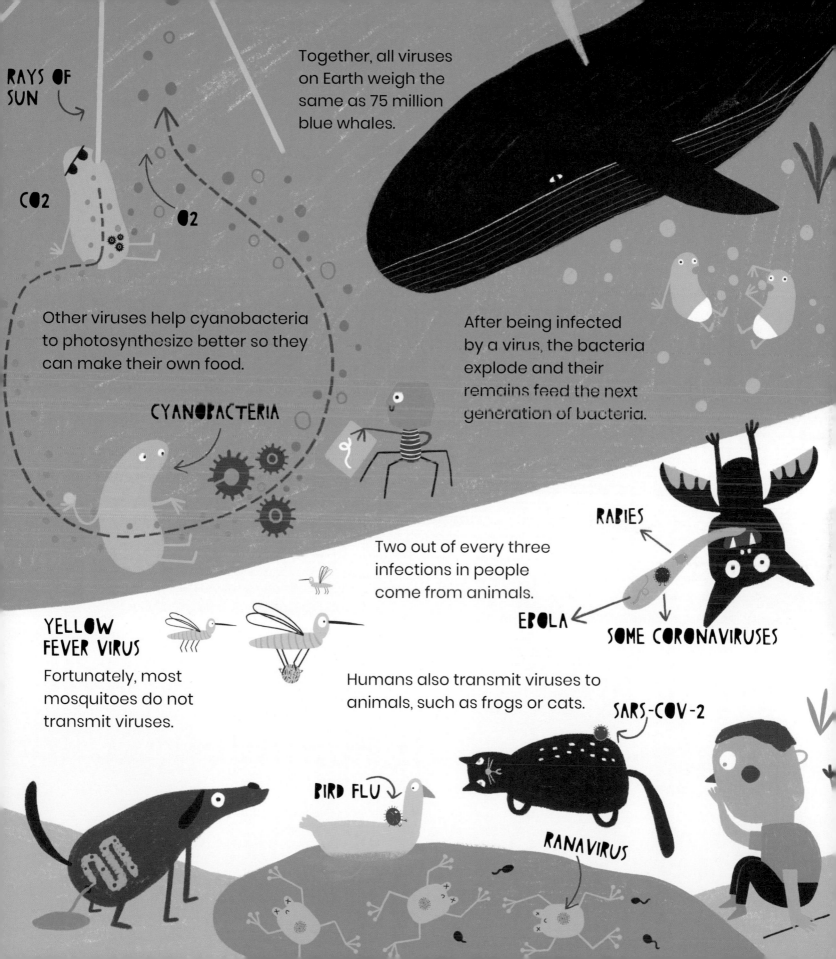

RAYS OF SUN

CO2

O2

Together, all viruses on Earth weigh the same as 75 million blue whales.

Other viruses help cyanobacteria to photosynthesize better so they can make their own food.

CYANOBACTERIA

After being infected by a virus, the bacteria explode and their remains feed the next generation of bacteria.

RABIES

Two out of every three infections in people come from animals.

EBOLA

SOME CORONAVIRUSES

YELLOW FEVER VIRUS

Fortunately, most mosquitoes do not transmit viruses.

Humans also transmit viruses to animals, such as frogs or cats.

SARS-COV-2

BIRD FLU

RANAVIRUS

A HISTORY OF VIRUSES IN HUMANS

Viruses existed on Earth long before humans. Viruses are known to have infected insects 300 million years ago.

300 BCE
Possible origin of smallpox in the Egyptian empire.

1100-1200 **CE
Origin of measles in the Middle East.

NEOLITHIC
(10,000 *BCE)

The first epidemics occur when the first settlements develop.

VARIOLA

MEASLES

These viruses later spread to Europe.

MIDDLE OF THE 20TH CENTURY

Many new vaccines are being developed.

1979
Defeat of smallpox, which killed about 300 million people in just the 20th century.

1964
June Almeida is the first person to see a coronavirus under an electron microscope.

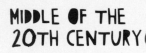

1980S TO TODAY
New animal viruses appear like HIV, Ebola, SARS, and coronavirus.

*BCE: before the common era

**CE: common era

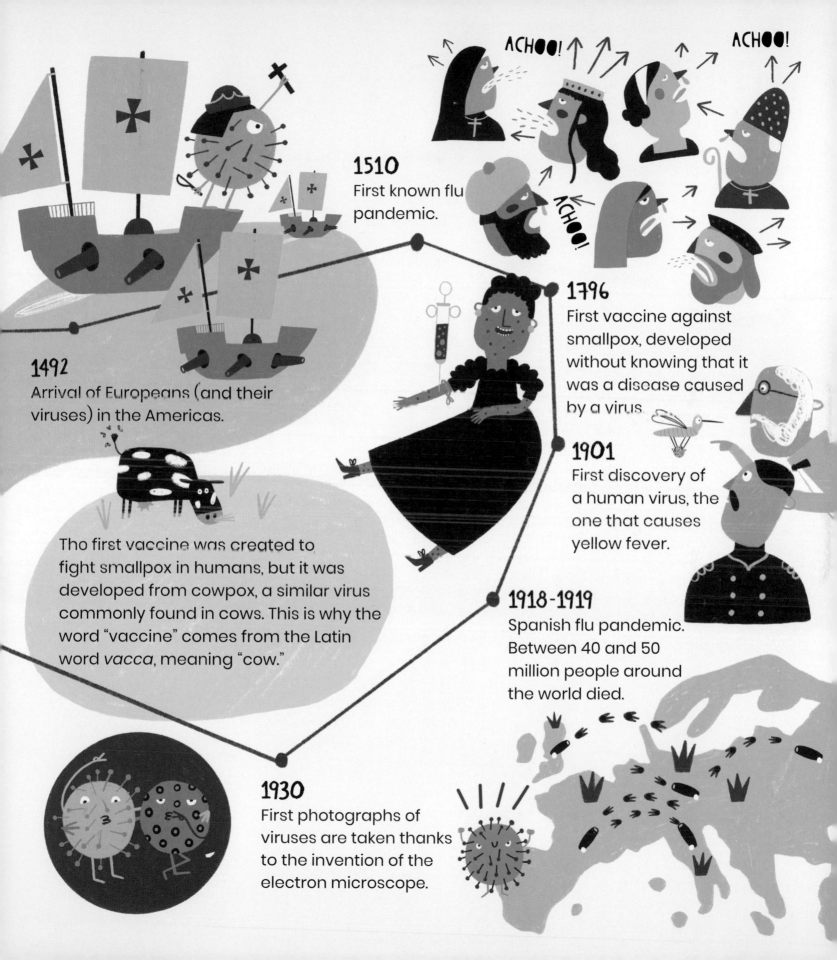

1510
First known flu pandemic.

1492
Arrival of Europeans (and their viruses) in the Americas.

The first vaccine was created to fight smallpox in humans, but it was developed from cowpox, a similar virus commonly found in cows. This is why the word "vaccine" comes from the Latin word *vacca*, meaning "cow."

1796
First vaccine against smallpox, developed without knowing that it was a disease caused by a virus.

1901
First discovery of a human virus, the one that causes yellow fever.

1918-1919
Spanish flu pandemic. Between 40 and 50 million people around the world died.

1930
First photographs of viruses are taken thanks to the invention of the electron microscope.

ACHOO!

ACHOO!

ACHOO!

TRUE OR FALSE?

1 Each virus can only infect one species.

2 Antibiotics don't fight against viral infections.

3 It is possible to defeat a virus.

4 Viruses can live on different surfaces.

5 All viruses cause disease in humans.

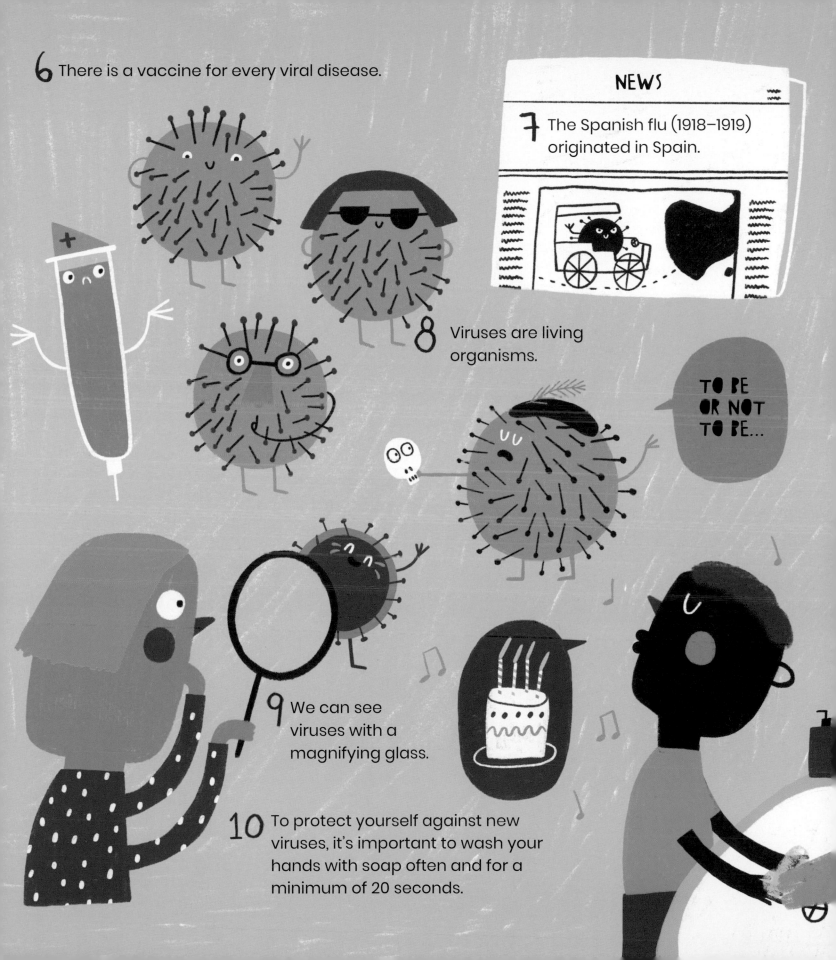

6 There is a vaccine for every viral disease.

NEWS

7 The Spanish flu (1918–1919) originated in Spain.

8 Viruses are living organisms.

TO BE OR NOT TO BE...

9 We can see viruses with a magnifying glass.

10 To protect yourself against new viruses, it's important to wash your hands with soap often and for a minimum of 20 seconds.

A HEALTHY WORLD

Our health is connected to the health of animals and the environment. If we protect our planet, we also protect ourselves.

With increasing globalization, the spread of viruses can be difficult to stop.

But there are a lot of things **YOU** can do:

1 FOLLOW THE RECOMMENDATIONS OF SCIENTISTS AND HEALTH PROFESSIONALS because they are the ones who know viruses best.

2 LEAVE WILD ANIMALS IN THEIR NATURAL HABITAT

Capturing or keeping wild animals such as monkeys and bats can cause new viruses to reach humans. This is what happened with the HIV, Nipah, and SARS viruses.

3 PROTECT THE FORESTS

The jungles and forests are the habitat of wild animals. If we cut down the trees, we increase our contact with these animals and make it easier for new viruses to jump to humans.

4 USE LOCAL AND SUSTAINABLE PRODUCTS

Keeping lots of livestock all together in one place can lead to the spread of swine flu and bird flu in humans. Large-scale farming can contribute to the spread of viruses like West Nile and Nipah. Smaller local farms and sustainable companies often avoid practices like these, which helps keep us all safer from viruses!

5 TAKE CARE OF YOUR PERSONAL HYGIENE

(but don't obsess over it!) As you already know, not all viruses are bad, only some. By staying clean and healthy, you can protect yourself and others against the bad viruses.

6 BECOME AN ENVIRONMENTAL DEFENDER

Ticks and mosquitoes (and the viruses they carry) are spreading into more and more areas due to global warming. Air pollution makes us more prone to viral infections.

NATURE NEEDS YOU

7 TAKE CARE OF THE SEAS AND OCEANS

so viruses and other small organisms can do their jobs and keep the environment balanced.

ANSWERS

1 Viruses reproduce very quickly, which allows them to mutate rapidly and jump from one species to another.

2 Antibiotics are only helpful against bacterial infections. The misuse of antibiotics increases bacteria's resistance to them, creating superbugs that can no longer be eliminated by antibiotics.

3 Thanks to mass vaccination campaigns all over the world, the virus that causes smallpox and poliovirus types 2 and 3 have been eliminated from the entire human population. We're working on defeating other viruses too.

4 Although viruses need living hosts in which to reproduce, they can live for several hours or even days on surfaces such as plastic, wood, or paper.

5 There are viruses everywhere on Earth, including in Antarctica and the oceans, but only a very small fraction cause disease in humans.

6 Some viruses are so complicated or mutate so fast that it is very difficult or even impossible to develop a vaccine against them.

7 It was called the "Spanish flu" because Spain was the first country to report the disease. Many of the other countries that were affected were busy fighting in World War I, so their newspapers were slower to report on the deadly flu.

8 Viruses cannot survive without a cell to reproduce, unlike living organisms. However, scientists are still debating the exact definition of "life."

9 Viruses are so small that you need a very special microscope, called an electron microscope, to see them.

10 Soap dissolves the lipid coat of the virus. Sing "Happy Birthday" twice while you wash your hands to make sure 20 seconds have passed.

First published in the United States in 2021 by Sourcebooks
Text © 2020, 2021 by Drs. Anna Cabré Albós, Laura García Ibáñez, Blanca Bernal,
Adriana Humanes, Ana Payo Payo and Alicia Pérez-Porro
Illustrations © 2020, 2021 by Mariona Tolosa Sisteré
Internal design © 2020, 2021 by Zahorí de Ideas
Cover design by Allison Sundstrom/Sourcebooks

English translation © 2021 by Sourcebooks

Published by Sourcebooks eXplore, an imprint of Sourcebooks Kids

P.O. Box 4410, Naperville, Illinois 60567–4410
(630) 961-3900
sourcebookskids.com

Originally published as *La vida secreta dels virus* in 2020 in Spain by Zahorí de Ideas.

Library of Congress Cataloging-in-Publication Data is on file with the publisher.

Source of Production: 1010 Printing Asia Limited, Kwun Tong, Hong Kong, China
Date of Production: March 2022
Run Number: 5025815

Printed and bound in China.
OGP 10 9 8 7 6 5 4 3 2

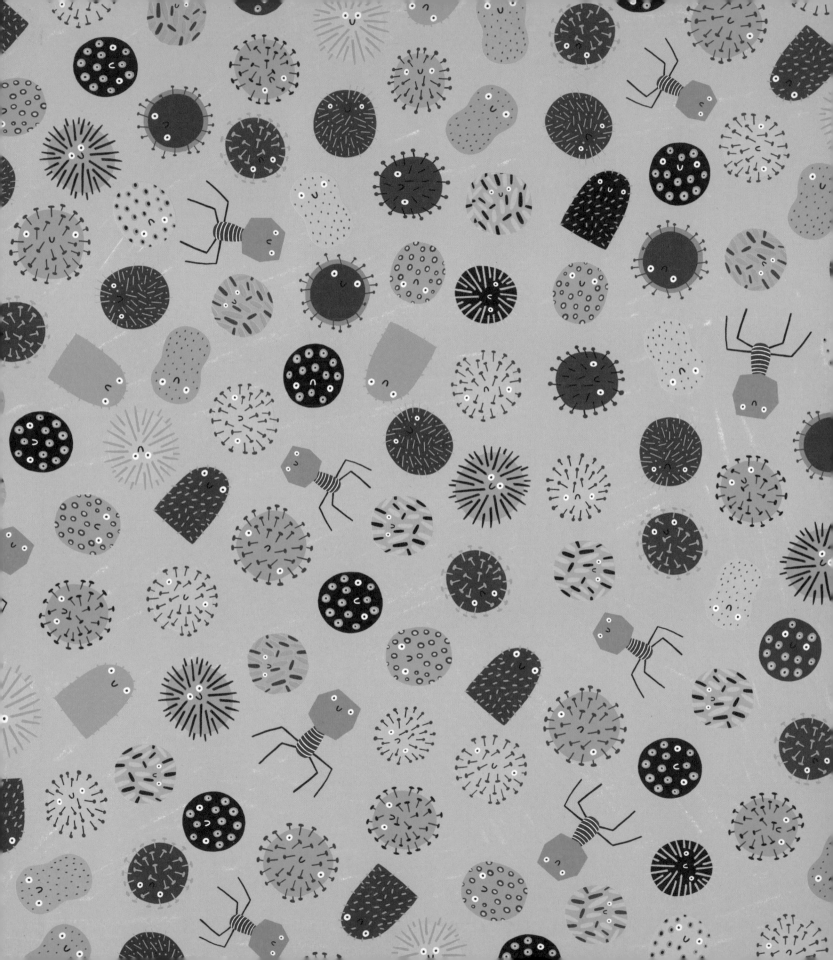